MAKE MONEY FAST!
DRIVE WOMEN WILD!

YOU CAN'T EXPECT TO HOLD A WOMAN *if you lack masculine vitality!*

MAKE MONEY FAST!
DRIVE WOMEN WILD!

and other offers
too good to refuse
from the small ads

Pete Alexander

EBURY
PRESS

1 3 5 7 9 10 8 6 4 2

First published 2002 by Ebury,
an imprint of Random House,
20 Vauxhall Bridge Road, London SW1V 2SA
www.randomhouse.co.uk

Random House Australia (Pty) Limited
20 Alfred Street, Milsons Point, Sydney,
New South Wales 2061, Australia

Random House New Zealand Limited
18 Poland Road, Glenfield, Auckland 10, New Zealand

Random House South Africa (Pty) Limited
Endulini, 5A Jubilee Road, Parktown 2193, South Africa

The Random House Group Limited Reg. No. 954009

Printed and bound in Great Britain by
Biddles Ltd, Guildford and King's Lynn

A CIP catalogue record for this book is available from the British Library

ISBN 0 09 188511 6

CONTENTS

vi

A SPOT-ON FORMULA FOR SUCCESS

When I was a kid, like lots of others, I suffered from spots. One day, tucked away at the back of a comic, I came across a small advertisement that seemed to know all about me and my problem. It confirmed my anxiety about why girls were avoiding me like the plague, but offered a miracle solution. Suitably convinced, I quietly saved up enough pocket money (bad skin wasn't something you discussed with your mum or dad) and sent away by mail to a box number located in a London street that was difficult to find on any map. Several weeks later the magic cure arrived. I applied a yellow lotion to my face (the smell of which I'll never forget) and waited. And waited. Of course nothing happened, but by that time I had been parted from my hard-earned money and the scam was a success, even if my love life wasn't.

The spots eventually departed along with my adolescence, and although girls did not exactly come running in my direction, my interest in such tempting, intriguing but ultimately deceptive small ads had been aroused. In the future I was to be tempted again by among other things The Erectorscope, The Ventrilo, X-Ray Specs and Vice Spice. In my teens I also came close to taking up the challenge of the most famous small ad of all – Charles Atlas and his offer to make me into a hulking brute with a six-pack intimidating enough to scare off any other predatory male on the beach.

Most of the small ads featured in this book are drawn from American and British magazines and comics spanning the period from the 1920s, when the pulp magazines first proliferated, to the 1960s. Some were conceived in an earlier era but the advertisers continued to reprint those where the formula worked. It was an era with little regulation compared to today and 'entrepreneurs' of varying degrees of shadiness prospered. Peddling a cornucopia of

BOYS! THROW YOUR VOICE

Into a trunk, under the bed or anywhere. Lots of fun fooling teacher, policeman or friends.

THE VENTRILO

a little instrument, fits in the mouth out of sight, used with above for Bird Calls, etc. Anyone can use it. Never fails. A 64-page Book on Ventriloquism and the Ventrilo. ALL FOR 10c POSTPAID.

products from sex, in all its many forms, bizarre inventions and novelty devices to more abstract concepts like luck, magic and success, the smart operator lay in wait in escapist publications knowing that they had the lonely, the unfulfilled and, hopefully, the gullible as a captive audience. The ads play on fears as much as they provoke desires – spotty teenagers and sexual inadequates, the old and the ugly all had the finger pointed at them. Eventually government stepped in with legislation to

give the public some protection against themselves and small ads of this kind have largely become a thing of the past.

Some of the ads are taken from popular US publications like *Collier's Weekly*, *The Saturday Evening Post* and *Harper's Magazine* and their British counterparts, *Pearson's Weekly*, *The Strand* and *The Windsor Magazine*. But the majority are from the more sensational American pulps including *Spicy Adventures, Weird Tales* and *Black Mask* (the original home of hard-boiled detective fiction). Stimulated by the editorial content of these magazines, readers' dreams of something out of the ordinary beyond their humdrum lives were catered for by page after page of offers "Too Good to be Missed!" – exotic hobbies, erotic fantasies, bizarre gadgets and instant cure-alls. By the Second World War these ads had also found their way into the perfect feeding-grounds of kids' comics and the formative glamour magazines like *Photoplay* and *Tit-Bits*.

Originally crammed together in single columns amid acres of text and evocatively described as a "two-dimensional street market", these ads vied for the attention of the passing eye by every means possible. Their tone ranges from the curiously mock scientific to the comic and utterly ridiculous.

With many of the ads, if you took the time to read them properly you could see that the whole thing was a carefully worded 'sting' from the off. The problem was that people, for whatever reasons, wanted to believe them.

The success of the small ad lay in its minimalism. In some ways the less the reader has to go on the more his imagination runs wild, filling in the blank spaces with his own desires. The fact than they were hidden away too, made people feel like they had discovered something that others had missed – something so special and illicit that it could only be talked about in muted tones. Many of the ads mask exactly what they were selling with innuendo and insinuation, no doubt hoping that the reader would put two and two together to make five. An ad that seemed to be selling pornography could turn out to be pictures of fine art or innocent *National*

Geographic-style anthropology. But in an age when certain lifestyle choices were still frowned upon, the anonymity of goods by mail order in a plain package marked personal was many people's only embarrassment free route to what they desired. Most inviting of all to a young man in the Fifties, was the thought of receiving condoms by post and to be free from the smirks and titters that greeted your red-faced request at the local chemist or barbers.

Looking at these ads now, they have a curious innocence and an undeniable comic charm, particularly when compared to the more insidious and sophisticated shysterism at work in advertising today. These old black and white works of art now offer more than enough entertainment value for their familiar claim – "Satisfaction Guaranteed!" – to be finally true.

GET IN SHAPE
THE EASY WAY!

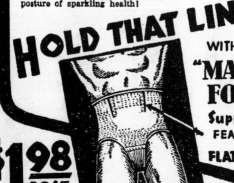

4

5

6

AND TO THINK THEY USED TO CALL ME SKINNY

Y-E-A SKINNY

SKINNY? NEW EASY WAY ADDS POUNDS

– so fast you're amazed

Astonishing gains with new double tonic. Richest imported ale yeast now concentrated 7 times, iron added. Gives 5 to 15 lbs. in a few weeks

DOCTORS for years have prescribed yeast to build up health. But now with this new discovery you can get far greater tonic results than with ordinary yeast—regain health, and also put on pounds of firm, handsome flesh—*and in a far shorter time.*

Not only are thousands quickly gaining good-looking pounds, but also clear skin, new pep.

Concentrated 7 times

This amazing new product, Ironized Yeast, is made from specially cultured *brewers' ale yeast* imported from Europe—the richest yeast known—which by a new process is concentrated 7 times—*made 7 times more powerful.*

But that is not all! This super-rich yeast is then *ironized* with 3 kinds of strengthening iron.

Day after day, as you take Ironized Yeast, watch flat chest develop, skinny limbs get husky, skin clear—you're a new person.

Results guaranteed

No matter how skinny and weak you may be, this marvelous new Ironized Yeast should build you up in a few short weeks as it has thousands. If not delighted with the results of the very first package, money back instantly.

Special FREE offer!

To start you building up your health *right away*, we make this FREE offer. Purchase a package of Ironized Yeast at once, cut out the seal on the box and mail it to us with a clipping of this paragraph. We will send you a fascinating new book on health, "New Facts About Your Body," by an authority. Remember, results are guaranteed with the very first package—*or money refunded.* At all good druggists. Ironized Yeast Company, Inc., Dept. 744, Atlanta, Ga.

Posed by professional models

8

HEY!
YOU FOLKS WITH NATURALLY SKINNY BUILDS!

Here's a Quick Way to put on 10 to 15 lbs. of Good Solid Flesh and Feel Like a Million Dollars!

Kelpamalt, the New Mineral Concentrate From the Sea— Rich in Newer Form of NATURAL IODINE—Guarantees 5 Lbs. in 1 Week or No Cost

MEN AND WOMEN EVERYWHERE AMAZED AT RESULTS

Thousands of thin, pale, rundown folks—and even "Naturally Skinny" men and women—are amazed at this new easy way to put on healthy needed pounds quickly. Gains of 15 to 20 lbs. in one month, 5 lbs. in 1 week, are reported regularly.

Kelpamalt, the new mineral concentrate from the sea, gets right down to the cause of thin, underweight conditions and adds weight through a "2 ways in 1" natural process.

First, its rich supply of easily assimilable minerals stimulates the digestive glands which produce the juices that alone enable you to digest fats and starches, the weight-making elements in your daily diet. And these minerals are needed by virtually every organ and for every function of the body. Second, Kelpamalt is rich in NATURAL IODINE—a mineral needed by the vital organ which regulates metabolism —the process through which the body is constantly building firm, solid flesh, new strength and energy. 6 Kelpamalt tablets contain more NATURAL IODINE than 486 lbs. of spinach or 1660 lbs. of beef. More iron and copper than 2 lbs. of spinach or 15 lbs. of fresh tomatoes. More calcium than 1 doz. eggs. More phosphorus than 3 lbs. of carrots.

9

10

EVERY
WOMAN
DESERVES
A BEAUTIFUL
BOSOM

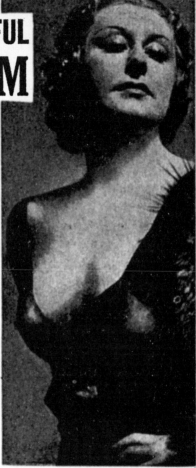

14

15

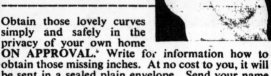
16

17

18

BOYS!
I'LL MAKE
A MAN OF YOU!

20

EARLE LIEDERMAN—The Muscle Builder

Author of "Muscle Building," "Science of Wrestling," "Secrets of Strength," "Here's Health," "Endurance," etc.

DO LADIES LOVE BRUTES ?

Women want he-men for their husbands and sweethearts. None of this chorus-man stuff for the real girl. She wants to be proud of his physical make-up; proud of his figure in a bathing suit. She knows that it's the fellow that is full of pep and vitality that gets ahead in this world. He's got the physical backbone to back-up the mental decisions he makes. He'll win out every time.

Send for my *Muscular Development* New Book **64 Pages and —IT'S FREE**

VALUABLE HINTS

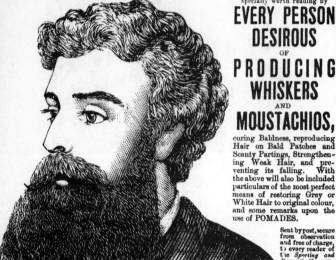

22

NOW SCIENCE KNOWS WHY

You Lose Hair and Go

BALD

BLIND TO HIS GREATEST HANDICAP!

READ FREE OFFER!

Germs get deep into the scalp skin and are not removed with soap and water, shampoos, hair tonics, salves and oils. These germs (*flask bacilli of Unna*) create fine dandruff to clog up pores and hair follicles, causing itch, falling hair and smothering the roots so they cannot grow hair. So why hide your bald parts with your hat, when a new method enables men to easily remove the thin, congested, germ-laden outer layer of scalp skin and have a new outer layer that will absorb air, sunshine and benefit from stimulating, nourishing preparations to activate the dormant roots to function and promote hair growth. This new method is now explained in a treatise called "HOW HAIR GROWS" and tells what to do. It is being mailed absolutely free to all who have hair troubles. Write to Dermolav Lab., Desk 400-M, No. 1700 Broadway, N. Y. You receive it by mail postpaid. If pleased tell friends.

EASY WAY....
Tints Hair
JET BLACK

This remarkable CAKE discovery, TINTZ Jet Black Shampoo, washes out dirt, loose dandruff, grease, grime and safely gives hair a real smooth JET BLACK TINT that fairly glows with life and lustre. Don't put up with faded dull, burnt, off color hair a minute longer. TINTZ Jet Black Cake works gradual . . . each shampoo leaves your hair blacker, lovelier, softer, easier to manage. No dyed look. Won't hurt permanents. Full cake 50c (3 for $1). TINTZ comes in Jet Black, light, medium and dark Brown, Titian, and Blonde. Order today! State shade wanted.

SEND NO MONEY
Just pay postman plus postage on our positive assurance of satisfaction in 7 days or your money back. (We Pay Postage if remittance comes with order.) Don't wait — Write today to TINTZ COMPANY, Dept. 878, 207 N. MICHIGAN, CHICAGO. CANADIAN OFFICE: Dept. 878, 22 COLLEGE STREET, TORONTO

23

HAVE A NEW SKIN!

Read this
Free Offer
IN 3 DAYS

25

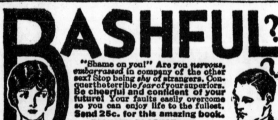
28

CIGARS DE JOY FOR **ASTHMA & BRONCHITIS**

One of these Cigarettes gives IMMEDIATE RELIEF in the worst attack of ASTHMA, HAY FEVER, CHRONIC BRONCHITIS, INFLUENZA, COUGH, and SHORTNESS OF BREATH, and their daily use effects a COMPLETE CURE. Persons who suffer at night with COUGHING, PHLEGM, and SHORT BREATH, find them invaluable, as they instantly check the spasm, promote sleep, and allow the patient to pass a good night.

Price 2s. 6d. per box of 35, and may be obtained of all Chemists, or, post free, from WILCOX & CO., 239, OXFORD STREET, LONDON, on receipt of Stamps or P.O.O. NONE GENUINE UNLESS SIGNED ON BOX, E. W. WILCOX.

HAVE YOU A RED NOSE ?

Send an envelope (stamped and addressed), and you will learn how to permanently rid yourself of such a terrible affliction free of charge. Send no money. Address in confidence :

A. K. TEMPLE, Specialist,
39, MADDOX ST., REGENT ST., LONDON, W.

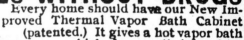

FALSE TEETH

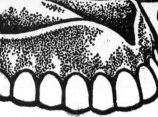

60 DAYS TRIAL

I have thousands of satisfied customers all over the country who could not afford to pay big prices. I have been making dental plates for many years, by mail. I guarantee you satisfaction or they do not cost you one cent, and I take your word. Teeth made especially for you personally can be tried for sixty days. In one Pennsylvania town alone, 91 people are wearing teeth made by me. They are satisfied and saved money.

SEND NO MONEY

My plates are very beautiful to look at and are constructed to give life-long service and satisfaction. You can look younger at once. They are made with pearly white genuine porcelain teeth. Well fitting and guaranteed unbreakable. Remember you do not send one cent—just your name and address, and we send

FREE free impression material and full detailed directions. Be sure to write today for my low prices and complete information. Don't put this off. Do it today.

DR. S. B. HEININGER, D. D. S.
440 W. Huron St., Dept. 1072, Chicago, Illinois

MEN GO WILD

about splendid teeth. Therefore, fair ladies, it behoves you to know that **Sozodont** makes them glitter like Orient pearl. By this pure Vegetable Dentifrice the enamel is rendered impervious to decay, all discolourations are removed, the gums become hard and rosy, and the *breath* pure and sweet. No lady ever used **Sozodont** without approving of its cleansing and purifying properties, and the flattering testimonials that have been bestowed upon it by eminent Dentists and scientific men speak volumes of praise for its merits. **Sozodont** contains not one particle of acid or any ingredient whatever that will injure the enamel, and is free from the acrid properties of Tooth Paste, &c. One bottle of **Sozodont** will last six months. Sold by Chemists, 2s. 6d. British Dépôt : 46, Holborn Viaduct, London, E.C.

33

WEAK MEN Suffering from the effects of **Youthful Errors, Early Decay, Loss of Manhood and Memory, Depression of Spirits, Disturbed Rest, Blushing, Loss of Flesh,** and a general breaking-up of the Physical and Mental Organisation, **SHOULD CONSULT**

Dr. Hirst, U.S.
33, Cross Hills,
HALIFAX.

Read this Remarkable Cure of Nervous and Physical Debility:

To Dr. Hirst.—Dear Sir, I write this to express my gratitude to you for the service you have rendered me in my affliction. It is six months since I first called upon you for advice ; prior to that time I had suffered over three years from the above. When I called, my system was well-nigh broken down, my memory was impaired, the bowels refused to act, I also suffered from Piles, but after the space of two months a rapid change took place, and to-day, I feel stronger and better than I have done for years. I remain, yours truly, CURED.

Full name and address given to anyone on application

Established 1850. **ADVICE FREE.** Ten years in present premises.

35

36

WHAT A PITY!

Yet she could banish her SUPERFLUOUS HAIR entirely!

IF you suffer from this terrible scourge which sometimes afflicts otherwise beautiful women there is yet hope. If you will only listen to the amazing experience of Mrs. Hudson. She was the popular wife of a young Officer in India until life was made utterly miserable for her by dreadful disfiguring growths of hair which completely ruined her charms and made her shun the company of her former friends. Then her husband, through the gratitude of a Hindoo soldier whose life he had saved, learnt the secret which keeps the Hindoo women's skin so smooth and free from all traces of hair. He brought the glad news to his wife, who tried the remedy more in despair than with any hope of success. To her amazement, she found that in a short time her skin was smooth and white and every sign of superfluous hair had vanished. Now no one will believe that she once suffered from such a disfiguring affliction. In her gratitude for her miraculous relief, Mrs. Hudson decided to make known the remedy to other women who are troubled with unwanted hair.

If you will just send the coupon and three penny stamps to Mrs. Hudson (Room D.3), No. 9 Old Cavendish Street, London, W.1, she will pass on the details to you, and you will be rid of your affliction.

THIS COUPON or copy of same to be sent with your name and address and threepence in stamps. Mrs. Hudson—Please send me your full information and instructions to cure superfluous hair. Address — Frederica Hudson (Room D.3), No. 9 Old Cavendish Street, London, W.1.

IMPORTANT NOTE.—Mrs. Hudson belongs to a family high in Society and is the widow of a prominent Army Officer, so you can write her with every confidence to the above address, where she has been established since 1916.

99 WOMEN out of 100 DON'T NEED DEODORANTS!

Not now! Today there's news of a much better idea. It's new LINC-O-LIN all-over Skin Perfume Spray and it does away with the need for a deodorant!

LADY LUCK
WILL SMILE ON YOU

40

42

Send 6d. for the History and a S.A.E. to Joan the Wad, Joan's Cottage, Lanivet, Cornwall. Thousands say :—

SHE HAS THE SECRET

In several million booklets you may read extracts from testimonials received from us far back as 1930. We just take them at random. We possess more than **Twelve Thousand** unsolicited testimonials, and we know from chance remarks that many who swear by Joan, never trouble to report to us. Having so many we can't possibly publish them all, nor can we constantly be changing our advertisements and we have been content to keep to those originally published, but such is the immense interest being displayed we thought we would depart from our rule in a small measure and just publish 6 or 7 of the huge number that came in during 1945. Remember similar testimonials have been coming in unceasingly since 1930.

DOCTOR GAVE UP HOPE—CURED—BETTER HEALTH.
" Dear Joan the Wad. Since I received you a few months ago I have had lots of luck. First of all I had to come into hospital with an Osteomyitis leg. The doctor gave up hopes of my recovery but after I was sent home I then sent to you, for a Joan the Wad and believe me I started to get well again and now I am back again in hospital as one leg had grown longer than the other. I then brought Joan in with me. I carried her to the operating theatre table and the bone was taken away from my thigh and my operation has proved a success. Next my knee has been straight for three years, now with exercise and massage it is starting to bend. I am sure that Joan the Wad has brought me lots of luck. If ever anyone says in here I'm always unlucky I always say for Joan the Wad. Wherever I go I will recommend her. I do hope you accept my story as I am a great believer in her. Yours sincerely, P. H., Sturges Ward, Wingfield Hospital, Oxford. 10.12.45."

NEVER WITHOUT MONEY.
" I received one of your Histories about three weeks' ago and it has brought me luck. Before I received your book I was always without money, but now thanks to you I am never without money ! (Mrs.) G. O., Glos. 8.10.45."

HOMELESS
LOOKED FOR A HOUSE FOR FOUR YEARS—Got Joan. Got a House, Got a job as well.
" . . . Believe it or not Things have taken an astonishing change for the better since the day I received Joan—more than I have dared hope for before. I am being discharged from Services, Oct. 22nd. My family are homeless and I couldn't take a job. But now I have offered me a job with a cottage and good wages, one of my favourite jobs, tractor driving. Please note I have been after a house for just on four years. G. S., Army Fire Service, Slough. 10.10.45."

INCREASE IN WAGES.
" . . . already after one fortnight we have had luck. I won . . . sum of £30 . . . also have got £1 per week increase in wages unexpected so Joan the Wad must be our lucky Star. So please send Jack O'Lantern to make the pair complete. (Mrs.) D. M., Kirkgate, Leeds. 19.11.45."

LOST HIS JOAN—LOST HIS LUCK.
" Please let me know how much to send for Joan the Wad and Jack O'Lantern. I had them both in 1931, but somehow lost them in hospital two years ago. I can honestly say that since losing them nothing has seemed to go right with me. I know what good luck Joan can bring by honest facts I have really experienced. . . . I certainly know that Joan the Wad is more than a lucky charm. Mr. E. E. S., Liphook, Hants 10.11.45."

MARRIED A MILLIONAIRE.
" . . . two of my friends have won £500 each since receiving your mascots and another has married an American millionaire. . . . Please forward me one Joan the Wad and one Jack O'Lantern. C. H., Levenshulme. 3.11.45."

BETTER JOB, MORE MONEY, LESS HOURS, IMPROVED HEALTH.
" My dear Joan . . . She has brought me continual good luck and her influence spreads to every sphere . . . I have got a much better job . . . greater wages . . . less working hours . . . and my health has greatly improved. I have always been a lonely kind of person, but . . . a friend of the opposite sex, she is also lonely . . . great opportunity for comradeship offered. So you see how the influence of Joan works. My pockets have always been full and I have had many wishes and desires fulfilled . . . I would not part with Joan for her weight in gold, she is much too valuable in every way. Her powers extend all over the world, and she works unceasingly for the full benefit of her friends and adherents. She rides in my pocket day and night and never leaves me. . . . D. H., Leeds, 9. 2.11.45."

All you have to do is to send a 6d. stamp and a stamped addressed envelope for the history to

167, JOAN'S COTTAGE, LANIVET, BODMIN

44

46

LOVE DROPS

AND RUBBER GOODS
BY POST

49

51

52

FRENCH LOVE DROPS

(Essence of Ecstasy)

Like a gift from fairyland, its exquisite scent surrounds you with the much desired atmosphere of alluring charm. Attracted by its delicate fragrance, young and old quickly surrender to its persuasive influence.

To quickly introduce "Love Drops" we offer a full size vial for 98c., with confidential instructions how to use it most effectively. You also get absolutely free of charge a remarkabe Astrological chart of your sign. Send Money Order, check, bill or postal stamps. (C.O.D. orders, $1.37—plus shipping charges.)

French Roy—Box 131—Varick Sta., New York, N. Y., Dept. P.S.-1.

Please send me your "Love Drops" as per your offer.

54

WANT TO BE LOVED

Let me Dress your Stockings, Socks, Handkerchief, Slips, Gowns, Shorts, Undershirts, Bra, Panties, Garters, Girdles, Headcloths, Combs, Hairbrushes, Hats, Caps, Scarves, Sheets, Pillow Cases, Blankets, Quilts, Bath Cloths, Towels, Dishes, Spoons, Forks, Knives, Pots, Pans, Light Bulbs, Door Knobs, Locks, Keys, Auto Keys, Pictures, Candles, Pocket Mirrors, Earrings, Bracelets, Pens, Pencils, Writing Papers, Cosmetics, etc.

I'll Dress each item in MY POWERFUL ATTRACTING MAG-NETIC FLUID for 7 days and 7 nights and return them to you within 9 days. Start now to make people love you, admire you, respect you. Start now to influence people, control people, attract people of your desire. Society people are relying upon MY POWERFUL ATTRACTING MAGNETIC FLUID.

Send yours now and start being more irresistable.
Send a donation of $5.00 or more with each item to cover processing, handling and shipping charges. A process is said to last and last for years.

None will be processed without a donation for each item. Send as many items you want to send. Be sure to send a donation of $5.00 or more with each item. Send now!

Send to: ANN JONES
624 S. Michigan Avenue, Chicago 5, Illinois

SENT
IN A
PLAIN
SEALED
WRAPPER

63

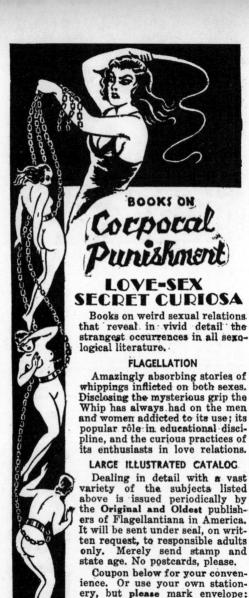

BOOKS ON
Corporal Punishment

LOVE-SEX SECRET CURIOSA

Books on weird sexual relations that reveal in vivid detail the strangest occurrences in all sexological literature.

FLAGELLATION

Amazingly absorbing stories of whippings inflicted on both sexes. Disclosing the mysterious grip the Whip has always had on the men and women addicted to its use; its popular rôle in educational discipline, and the curious practices of its enthusiasts in love relations.

LARGE ILLUSTRATED CATALOG

Dealing in detail with a vast variety of the subjects listed above is issued periodically by the **Original and Oldest** publishers of Flagellantiana in America. It will be sent under seal, on written request, to responsible adults only. Merely send stamp and state age. No postcards, please.

Coupon below for your convenience. Or use your own stationery, but please mark envelope:

THE GARGOYLE PRESS
Dept. DA-3
70 Fifth Avenue, New York, N. Y.

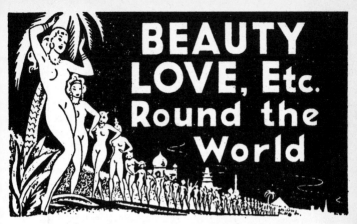

World's Greatest Collection of Strange & Secret Photographs

NOW you can travel round the world with the most daring adventurers. You can see with your own eyes, the weirdest peoples on earth. You witness the strangest customs of the red, white, brown, black and yellow races. You attend their startling rites, their mysterious practices. They are all assembled for you in these five great volumes of the **SECRET MUSEUM OF MANKIND.**

600 LARGE PAGES

Here is the World's Greatest Collection of Strange and Secret Photographs. Here are Exotic Photos from Europe, Harem Photos from Africa, Torture Photos, Female Photos, Marriage Photos from Asia, Oceania, and America, and hundreds of others. There are almost 600 LARGE PAGES OF PHOTOGRAPHS, each page 62 square inches!

1,000 REVEALING PHOTOS

You see actual love and courtship practiced in every quarter of the world. You see magic and mystery in queer lands where the foot of a white man has rarely trod. You see Oriental modes of marriage and female slavery in China, Japan, India, etc. Through the close-up of the camera you witness the exotic habits of every continent and female customs in America, Europe, etc. You are bewildered by ONE THOUSAND LARGE PHOTOGRAPHS, including 130 startling full-page close-ups, and thrilled by the hundreds of short stories that describe them.

5 PICTURE-PACKED VOLUMES

BOOK OF LOVE LETTERS

There is no greater or no more profound reality than love. There is no nobler possession than the love of another. There is no higher gift from one human being to another than love. The gift and the possession are true sanctifiers of life, and should

be worn as precious jewels, without affectation and without bashfulness. For this reason there is nothing to be ashamed of in a love letter, provided it be sincere. A celebrated writer once said that "to write a good love letter, you must begin without knowing what you are going to say, and finish without knowing what you have said." The remark is to some extent correct, as the true secret of all successful letter-writing lies in the power of conveying the thoughts, feeling and desires of the writer to his or her correspondent. Such a letter would undoubtedly reflect the state of the writer's heart, agitated and disordered by the tumultuous throbs of passion; but, as the zeal of young persons generally, in matters affecting the heart, is very apt to outrun discretion, expression would unconsciously be given to absurd and foolish protestations, or to extravagant and romantic adulation of the object of attachment.

72

74

YOU TOO CAN BE A DETECTIVE!

Alone in the House

a woman is always in danger of being surprised by a robber, and is, in a moment, brought face to face with the responsibility of defending herself, her home and little ones. At such a time she needs to have at hand some **safe, reliable firearm**, for under such circumstances self-defence entirely justifies its use. The

FOREHAND

"Perfection" Revolver

is particularly adapted to just such cases. The **positive cylinder stop** and the **automatic hammer block** make **accidental discharge an impossibility**. A child could drive nails with it loaded and not discharge it! Made of all steel, no malleable iron. Weight 10 and 12 ozs. Length of barrel 2 and 3 in. Light, artistic, perfect. Retail price $4.00. Is it not worth this amount to feel

Protected !

If your dealer cannot supply you we'll sell you direct at same price ($4.00), cash with order; but ask him first, it's handier.

FOREHAND ARMS CO., Worcester, Mass.

Arrest Him, Officer!

I'LL HAVE COMPLETE FACTS ON THE OTHER FELLOW TONIGHT!

OPERATOR NUMBER 38

Follow This Man!

SECRET Service Operator No. 38 is on the job... *follow him* through all the excitement of his chase after the counterfeit gang. See how a crafty operator works. Tell-tale finger prints in the murdered girl's room that help him solve the great mystery! BETTER than fiction because every word is TRUE. No obligation. Just mail me the coupon and get—

FREE The Confidential Reports No. 38 Made to His Chief

And the best part of it all is this—it may open your eyes to the great opportunity for YOU as a well paid Finger Print Expert. This is a young, *fast-growing* profession. The kind of work you would like. Excitement! Thrills! Travel! *A regular monthly salary.* Reward money. *And remember:* graduates of this school HEAD 47% of *all* Identification Bureaus in the U. S. Quick! Mail the Coupon NOW and I'll send you these Free Confidential Reports!

INSTITUTE OF APPLIED SCIENCE
1920 Sunnyside Ave., Dept. 7462, Chicago, Illinois

THE "DEMON" defies detection. It is made entirely of metal, beautifully plated, and weighs under 3oz. No movement is too rapid for it—even the lightning flash itself. By merely pressing the trigger the photograph is taken, therefore no knowledge of photography is necessary, for, unlike other cameras, it requires no focussing, no stand, no dark slides, yet hundreds of plates can be carried and exposed in rapid succession.

The DEMON CAMERA can be used on the promenade, in law courts, churches, and railway carriages, also in breach of promise and divorce cases—in fact, at all awkward moments when least expected.

NOTE.—Apparatus, including plates, chemicals, and instructions, post free 5s. 6d. Extra dry plates 9d. per doz., or 6 doz. for 4s. Specimen "Demon" photographs free one stamp.

"Drayton House, Daventry.

"DEAR SIR,—I received the 'Demon' to-day, and can only say it is as good as a camera that cost me £10. Please send me some photographic catalogues, as many of my friends wish to purchase from you.

"AUBREY L. BOYD."

THE AMERICAN CAMERA CO.,
93, OXFORD STREET, W.
Also 397, 399, Edgware Road, London, W.

NOTE.—*All letters to Manager M Department, latter address.*

Detective Opera Glass
AN OPTICAL CURIOSITY

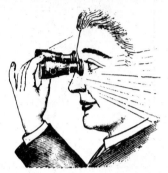

With the Detective Opera Glass you can see behind without turning your head. It is like having **EYES IN THE BACK OF YOUR HEAD**, and when people do not know you are looking you see some interesting sights sometimes.

No. 2776. Detective Opera Glass.
Price Postpaid.................... **35c**

THE
SEEBACKROSCOPE

Is a marvellous invention of science which enables you practically to

SEE OUT OF THE BACK OF YOUR HEAD,

It is only a tiny instrument made of polished ebonite, and easily carried in the waistcoat pocket, yet when fitted to the eye it enables you to watch undetected the movements of people following you in the street or seated behind you.

DETECTIVES USE IT.

THE WHOOPEE
CUSHION
AND OTHER AMAZING
NOVELTIES

Whoopee Cushion

The Whoopee Cushion or "Poo-Poo" Cushion, as it is sometimes called, is made of rubber. It is inflated in much the same manner as an ordinary rubber balloon and then placed on a chair, couch, seat, etc. When the victim unsuspectingly sits upon the cushion, it gives forth noises that can be better imagined than described. **BY MAIL POSTPAID.**
No. 2953. WHOOPEE CUSHION... **25c**

"NICOLAS"
or PUFF BILLIARDS.

The latest and most amusing indoor
game yet produced.

A STARTLING SHILLING NOVELTY.
THE YANKEE RUBBER BABY.

Goes in the Waistcoat pocket, blows out to life-size, is washable, durable, and unbreakable. Resembles life, for, like the real article, it coos at pleasure, yet screams awfully if smacked. Even experienced fathers are deceived by these laughter-producing infants, and no home can be a really happy one without their cheering presence.

In long White dress complete: Boys or Girls, 14 stamps. Twins, post free, 2s.

Address.—THE " FACSIMILEOGRAPH " COMPANY, Kemp Town, Brighton.

ITCHING POWDER

NOT MAILABLE

This is another good practical joke, the intense discomfiture of your victims to everyone but themselves, is thoroughly enjoyable. All that is necessary to start the ball rolling is to deposit a little of the powder on a person's hand and the powder can be relied upon to do the rest. The result is a vigorous scratch, then some more scratch, and still some more. Shipped by Express only.

No. 6257. ITCHING POWDER.... **10c**
3 boxes for 25 cents; 75c per dozen.

D.R.-Patent. a.

MIRACULOUS CIGAR - PIPE.

The Smoke produces charming pictures on small leaves in the tube. Amusing for every smoker and entertaining in society. Genuine Egriot Wood, 1s. 6d.; also for Cigarettes. Miraculous Tobacco Pipe, 1s. 6d. From two upwards post free to any address; from half-a-dozen upwards 20 per cent. discount. Postage stamps taken in payment.

HERMANN HURWITZ & CO.,
56, Basinghall Street, London, E.C.

THE RUBBER SMOKE BLOWER
A New and Original Novelty for Smokers

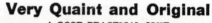

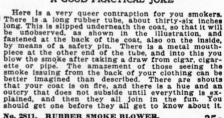

Very Quaint and Original
A GOOD PRACTICAL JOKE

Here is a very queer contraption for you smokers. There is a long rubber tube, about thirty-six inches long. This is slipped underneath the coat, so that it will be unobserved, as shown in the illustration, and fastened at the back of the coat, also on the inside, by means of a safety pin. There is a metal mouth-piece at the other end of the tube, and into this you blow the smoke after taking a draw from cigar, cigar-ette or pipe. The amazement of those seeing the smoke issuing from the back of your clothing can be better imagined than described. There are shouts that your coat is on fire, and there is a hue and an outcry that does not subside until everything is ex-plained, and then they all join in the fun. You should get one before they all get to know about it.

No. 2811. RUBBER SMOKE BLOWER.
Price Postpaid........................... 35c

Rubber Chewing Gum

This is an imitation of real chewing gum, five full size sticks to the pack. It is made of rubber, that is not likely to be distinguished from the real thing. A remarkable surprise to those that love the famous American exercise.

No. 2757. Rubber Chewing Gum... **10c**
3 packs for 25c., or 12 for 75c. postpaid

Do You Chew Gum?

Here is a little novelty every o
who loves to chew gum will appre
ate. "Peggy" is its name. "Peggy'
a convenient and handsomely de
rated tin box with a peg in the cen
to hold your gum when not in u
"Peggy" keeps the gum clean, co
healthful and handy. "Peggy" can
carried in the pocket, satchel or
tached to cord or chain. The m
"Peggy" is used the better it is lik
Mailed postpaid on receipt of 5 cen

Agents Wanted. THE PEGGY CO., Dep't D, Cincinnati

Joke Whiskey Bottle

Here's a great joke that fits in with the times. It's a regular whiskey bottle, filled with a liquid that closely resembles in appearance the "real stuff." However, as soon as the top is screwed off a large snake jumps out and the victim receives the surprise of his life. The bottle is so realistic that it will fool the most cautious.

Snake Whiskey Bottle

Imagine the fun you can have by pulling this bottle out of your pocket and offering your friends a drink. The result will bring more laughs than the funniest movie ever filmed. The bottle also comes in another style, with an exploding device in the cork. This cork is pulled out and as soon as it leaves the bottle a paper cap explodes with a loud bang. Another real joke device. With two of these bottles you can vary the fun and have no limit of entertainment.

The price of each style is ONLY 35 CENTS POST-PAID. Be sure to specify kind required when ordering.

Exploding Whiskey Bottle

PAPER CAPS can be supplied for the EXPLODING Whiskey Bottle at 10 cents per box, 3 boxes for 25 cents, or 75 cents per dozen boxes. Paper Caps, however, are not mailable, and are shipped by Express, not prepaid.

No. 2900. Snake Whiskey Bottle.... 35c

No. 2981. Exploding Whiskey Bottle 35c

90

WIFE BEATER

WHANG

The Wife Beater. Made of extra tough paper, corrugated and folded with riveted handle. Red, white and blue. When you slap with this it produces a loud, smacking noise; 13½ in. long. 1 dozen in bundle. **No. 26N9.**

Per gross **3.60**

Per dozen .... **.33**

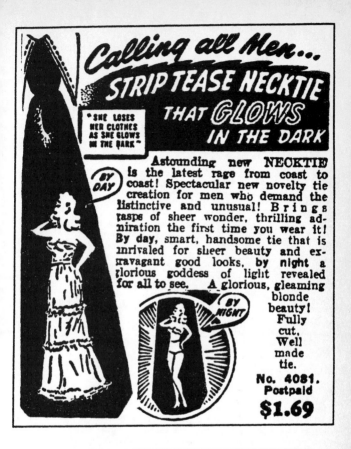
93

94

MY WORD!

Peek-A-Boos
HI-BALL GLASSES

WOW!

SHOCKING!

PUT LIFE IN YOUR PARTIES

Panic your guests! Serve drinks in new, smart PEEK-A-BOOS! A positive sensation! Each glass bears a pretty girl in a colorful costume. A turn of the glass reveals her life-like in Nature's own. Then peek through the liquid and see what happens! Daring! Funny! No home bar complete without them. An unusual gift. 6 subjects . . . all different. Also Peek-A-Boos in Whiskey, Cocktail and Pilsener styles! Order some now!

95

Delivers a Powerful but Harmless Electric Shock

It gives a powerful, yet harmless, electric shock that is guaranteed to wake 'em up. The Shocker is about 24 inches in length and about 1½ inches in diameter. Has wood handle and contact button right on handle grip. At other end is the "shocking contact." To operate you simply press the button and touch the tip to object.

For other effects, you can run wire from the contact point to chair, bed, cage, etc. or any other place you want to produce a shock. Then, at the right moment, press the button and the victim will get a JUICY SHOCK.

Constructed to provide dependable, trouble free service indefinitely. Nothing to go wrong. Makes rough handling of animals unnecessary—the sane way to handle them without doing them any injury. Has vacuum impregnated hot shot motor coil and large contact points on vibrator. Uses 4 standard flashlight batteries (not supplied) which insure hard shocking. Shock can be altered by using a different number o batteries.

No. 6030. ELECTRIC SHOCKER. . . . $6.95

No. 2548. Flashlight Batteries. Each. 10c

96

Hot Shot Electric Shocker

Loads of Fun... Many Practical Uses for this Shocking Prod

HOLDER STOCK PROD SURE MAKES 'EM MOVE EY?

YOU BET, SON - AND IT SAVES PLENTY OF MONEY

HOL-DEM STOCK PROD

Delivers a **POWERFUL, YET HARMLESS ELECTRIC SHOCK** that is **GUARANTEED TO MAKE 'EM MOVE FAST** whether they be **MAN OR BEAST.**

The **ELECTRIC PROD** was originally designed to be used to control animals on the farm, in the stock yards and for training purposes, but now practical jokesters have discovered that it makes one of the most sensational fun makers ever known. At a recent American Legion convention it literally "stole the show."

97

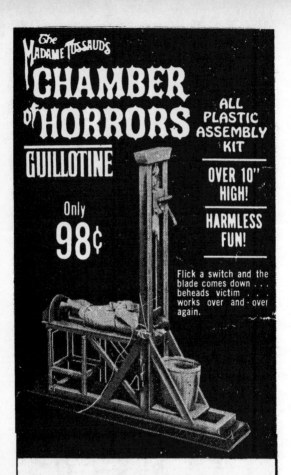

THE NAKED TRUTH
Magic Picture Card

Here is a perfectly new and wonderfully successful pocket novelty. When no one is thinking about "haves", snares or deceptions, you casually take from your pocket this Picture Card, which is exactly as illustrated, and you won't need to inquire whether anyone would like to see the remainder of the hidden figure, for their curiosity will be thoroughly aroused. The selected victim slides out the picture, and you have a real good laugh at his expense as he gets nicely "stung." This s a really good joke and catches the smartest of them.

No. 2135. Naked Truth. Price... **15c**
3 for 40 cents; $1.35 per doz. postpaid.

Comic Bald Head Rubber Mask

Change in seconds to "shiny" bald head. Look like old man. Fits over head above eyebrows, over forehead, around ears and back down to neck.

MAKE MONEY
AT HOME!

Easy as A-B-C

Here's a Queer Way to *Learn* Music!

BE YOUR own music teacher. Just a simple, easy, home-study method. Takes only a few minutes—averages only a few cents —a day. No "grind" or hard work. Every step is clear as crystal—simple as A-B-C throughout. You'll be surprised at your own rapid progress. From the start you are learning real *tunes* by note. Learn to play "jazz" or classical selections—right at home in your spare time.

Free Book and Demonstration Lesson

Don't be a wallflower. Send for Free Booklet and Free Demonstration lesson. These explain our wonderful home study method fully and show you how easily and quickly you can learn to play at little expense. Mention your favorite instrument. Instruments supplied when needed, cash or credit. Write NOW.

U. S. SCHOOL OF MUSIC
36710 Brunswick Bldg.,   New York City

Pick Your Instrument

Piano	Guitar
Violin	Saxophone
Organ	Mandolin
Cornet	Ukulele
Trombone	Harp
Piccolo	Clarinet
Flute	'Cello

Hawaiian Steel Guitar
Trumpet
Piano Accordion
Italian and German Accordion
Voice and Speech Culture
Harmony and Composition
Drums and Traps
Banjo (Plectrum, 5-String or Tenor)

104

MAGIC CHEESE CHIPS
OPPORTUNITY TO START
AN EXCEPTIONAL
BUSINESS at HOME

NO HOUSE-TO-HOUSE
Experience Unnecessary—No Costly Machine to Buy

You can work at home, chips come to you already made. A few moments work, put them in bags and they are ready to sell! No complicated work, no experience needed. No super-salesmanship or house-to-house canvassing. Stores do your selling for you. Magic Cheese Chips are big, crispy, fluffy, giant-size chips, bigger than potato chips. Delicious, tempting taste makes them act like an appetizer. Put a plateful on any store counter. People taste them and buy from clever "Silent Salesman" display. Decidedly unusual! Distributors ordering large quantities weekly.

A Tremendous Market Available

Here are the types of places where you may leave Magic Chip displays for the purpose of building up a good dealer business

Bathing Beaches	Theatres
Excursion Steamers	Department Stores
Amusement Parks	Hotel Lobbies
Carnivals	News Stands
Circuses	Bowling Alleys
Fairs	Billiard Halls
Golf Courses	Dance Halls
Roadstands	Train and Railroad Stations
Ballgrounds	Five and Ten Cent Stores
Soft Drink Stands	Fruit Stands
Grocers	Churches
Bakeries	Sandwich Shops
Confectioneries	Skating Rinks
Drug Stores	Restaurants

You Don't Invest a Red Cent

until you have sold yourself on the possibilities. We let you sell yourself first before you invest and our novel plan enables you to decide without paying for a single chip. Then you can start with $5.50 investment, put back your profits, building up without another penny investment, if you wish! *Money-back guarantee goes with initial purchase!*

Everything Furnished

We furnish everything — advertising, display stands, etc. Don't wait until it's too late! Write at once and get the exclusive rights for your locality. Samples and particulars free.

FLUFF-O-MFG. CO., Dept. 2038-G, St. Louis, Mo.

A Business of Great Promise

In its infancy now, but making exceptional progress. We are lining up distributors rapidly. Start now and grow with us! A delightful tidbit for parties, people munch them on the streets, at outdoor games, in restaurants, at the beaches in summer. Ideal item for beer taverns. Hundreds of open territories. Write today.

Send for Full Information

Convince yourself first that this is an unusual business with a real opportunity. No claims—you be the judge. Look into this now. No obligation. Mail the coupon immediately—later may be too late.

MAIL FOR COMPLETE DETAILS

**FLUFF-O MFG. CO.,
Dept. 2038-G, St. Louis, Mo.**

Without obligation to me, rush full information at once about Magic Cheese Chips and your proposition.

NAME ....

ADDRESS ....

....

Book of Great Secrets
One Thousand Ways of Getting RICH!

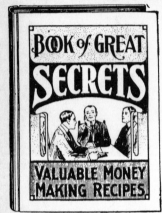

BOOK of GREAT SECRETS

VALUABLE MONEY MAKING RECIPES.

Large Collection of the Most Saleable Recipes and Formulas of Various Articles in Daily Use.

To persons who work hard for a living and then don't get it, we have a few plain words to say. Every person wants to make money and wants to make it fast and easy. This book will tell them how This is a large and very valuable collection of recipes and formulas for the manufacture of hundreds of articles in daily use, and which may be readily made by any one and sold at very large profits. Great fortunes have been made by the manufacture of single articles for which recipes are here given, and some of these recipes have been sold for as much as $50.00 each. Any one, by the aid of this book, can build up a steady, permanent and very profitable business, for there is constant demand for the various articles, they may be easily made by any one, and sold either wholesale or retail or through sub-agents. Many have started in life in just this way. Get this great book, and without doubt it will start you on the road to a competence.

SUMMARY OF CONTENTS:

SECRETS OF THE LIQUOR TRADE: How to make wines, beers and brandies, whiskies, ciders, champagne, rum, gin, and other hard and soft drinks. So complete is this chapter that its contents can better be judged by a few of the recipes it includes, such as making cider without apples, port wine, Madeira wine, brandy, cognac brandy, brandy bitters, Holland gin, cordial gin, Jamaica rum, Irish and Scotch whiskey, improved English strong beer, and many others. It also reveals the secret of correcting wine, beer and whiskey that seems to have spoiled, a feature that will well repay the home brewer should he come in contact with this trouble. Furthermore, it also tells how to give beer and other liquors the appearance of age.

DRUGGIST'S DEPARTMENT: How to make corn cures, cough compounds, digestive pills, numerous kinds of ointments that have been used for years in the treatment of various skin afflictions, foot ointments, tonics, health bitters and a time-tested treatment for the cure of drunkenness likewise is explained in detail. This chapter alone, many customers have told us, is worth the price of the book because of the extremely rare and valuable information it contains.

MANUFACTURER'S DEPARTMENT reveals the secrets of making all kinds of inks, furniture polish, various kinds of soaps, paste resembling diamonds, various kinds of cements and glues, how to make a cheap white house paint, an excellent substitute for inks, magic copying paper, steel annealing process; it tells how to soften cast iron for drilling, how to recut old files and rasps, how the Chinese repaired holes in iron, and many similar hitherto unknown facts.

TOILETRY, PERFUMERY, ETC., is a chapter that bares the secret of making hair restorer and hair dyes, of making a baldness cure, of making a depilatory for the removal of superfluous hair; it tells in detail also how to make face paint, how to make a liquid rouge for the complexion, how to make smelling salts, oil of roses for the hair; to make brown teeth white, and reveals dozens of other similar important and easily understood secrets.

FACE PAINTS: Full instructions for the making of face paints, rouge and other cosmetics.

HUNTERS' AND TRAPPERS' SECRETS are told in this chapter and many problems which the average hunter and trapper encounters in the course of his activity can be solved with a little study of its contents.

FARMERS' DEPARTMENT tells how to make a rat killer, a lotion for the mange, lotions for bruises, sprains and other injuries which cattle and horses may suffer and many similar remedies.

FINE ARTS AND SCIENCES is a chapter dealing with the art of transferring pictures on to glass; how to make wax flowers, etc., etc.

CONFECTIONER'S DEPARTMENT: Toffee, chocolate cream, candied lemon, etc., etc.

HOUSEHOLD AND EVERYDAY REQUIREMENTS deals with recipes and facts which every housewife and many others should know. It tells how to make vinegar, cider, chili sauce, how to keep hams, how to clean rugs and furniture, how to make eye water, tomato catsup and 84 additional useful household and everyday secrets.

CALICO PRINTER'S FAST DYES contains a description of 13 different colors, clearly explained, for fast colors.

DYES FOR BONE AND IVORY deals with this fascinating business and also varnishes, gilding, bronzing and more than 40 other secrets.

PRINTING INKS deals not only that subject but also paper copying and the art of inlaying and ornamenting papier mache.

REMEDIES FOR DISEASES OF HORSES chapter contains numerous formulae for treating the various diseases to which horses are subject and from which they often die because their symptoms are not properly understood.

The book is literally crammed full of recipes—nearly 100 pages of valuable money-making recipes, formulas, secrets, wrinkles, etc., any one of which that you make use of will be well worth many times the small cost of the book. Among the valuable secrets in this book are many that require little or no capital and but little labor, with no special ability.

No. 1250. **BOOK OF GREAT SECRETS. Price Postpaid to any Address...** **25c**

Now Comes the Startling Discovery of A Mysterious "MOONLIGHT RING"

Changes Nickles Into One-Dollar Bills
With Plan that Brings up to $14 a Day

MANY have said this marvelous ring is like the fabled ring of Arabia, which the wearer had only to rub and unlimited fortune would be his . . .Of course, such a ring only existed in the fantastic fairy tales of our youth. But, now a startling discovery by a hitherto obscure scientist has amazed society with a mysterious "Moonlight Ring" which has already PROVEN its ability to bring money to all who use its secret effectively. This modern "Magic Ring" is not based on superstition or "luck." Its power does not come from "Black Magic"—it is a scientific achievement which has taken years of effort and a fortune in money to develop.

A Marvelous Story

This ring is called the "MOON-LIGHT RING." Its discovery came about with the discovery of a new perfume—a **solidified** perfume which, when slightly heated, evaporates into the atmosphere, thus imparting a delicate, ex tic fragrance to an entire home or large room. It is **not** an incense. There is no burning smell—no smoke—no ashes! The secret formula is so clever that the delightful fragrance mingles almost instantly with all the air in the room; it does not just settle to the floor or rise to the ceiling.

The "Moonlight Ring"

Then came the discovery of the "Moonlight Ring"—a dainty hollow ring that slips on **any electric light bulb** and is concealed by even the smallest lamp shade . . . Into this ring is put the solidified perfume in the form of tiny, bright silver grains. The light is turned on. Within a moment the entire atmosphere of the room is charged with a mysterious, delicate, alluring fragrance of freshly cut

Not a "Luck Charm" — yet it has brought good fortune to hundreds . . . . Not a "Wishing Ring" — yet it may bring you what you most desire . . . . You give it away Free — yet you earn up to $14 A DAY

STEADY INCOME

flowers. An "aromatic symphony," as from a dewy garden, bringing romance and sparkle into even the most ordinary surroundings. Its seductive charms have captured refined society. Now they are pouring golden dollars into the pockets of men and women who are far-sighted enough to let its magic work money-making miracles for them.

Men and Women Making Up to
$14 A DAY
Giving Free Rings
With a Plan That Includes

Our new plan lets you give "MOON-LIGHT RINGS" away FREE. The customer does not have to buy anything to get them. Yet, we show you how to make up to $14 a day—get 50c for almost every one you hand out. No wonder Mrs. Burchard averaged $14 a day—Malone reports an average of $2.50 an hour—men and women taking in money easier than any way they ever tried before. In another 30 days this new sensation will have thousands held enthralled. Get in on the "ground floor" of a proposition that indicates within a month will be setting earnings records for all time.

FREE Rings Furnished You Free of Extra Charge. New Money - Making Plan Changes Buffalo Nickles to Dollar Bills.

Right now, when the world's greatest brains are working on plan for a greater distribution of wealth; while senators and financiers and even the President of the United States are calling on their genius to give people money—**this plan has developed!** Nothing like it before. Our secret plan tells people how to start out in the morning with 20 MAGIC RINGS and 20 Buffalo Nickels; shows how to hand them to 20 people and return in 2 hours with 20 one-dollar bills! Sounds too good to be true? Sounds impossible? **Test it yourself! We will pay you cash if it fails!** No "sleight of hand," no "short changing"— financiers have been amazed at it, but they agree that this stupendous plan works . . . It is impossible to let everyone in on this gold-scattering offer, so act at once! Have cash quick! Rush coupon for SAMPLE offer.

Illidela Corporation
Department 194
311 N. Des Plaines St., Chicago, Ill.

HOW TO WIN A
WATCH FREE.
ABSOLUTELY

WHAT PLACE IN ENGLAND DOES THIS PICTURE REPRESENT?

If correct you receive a **GRAND PRIZE** of a **SOLID SILVER WATCH**, timed for all Climates, and WARRANTED to be Superior to the one sold to us by an Ordinary Jeweller for £2 12s. 6d.

Our only conditions are that you send us the answer with a stamped addressed envelope for us to write and tell you if you are correct, and that, when the Watch is sent, you also order to be sent with it one of our Silver Chains, as per our unprecedented offer, which we will send.

ADDRESS:

Watchmakers' Alliance, 184, Oxford St. London

Endorsed by the Press of England.
" Perfectly honest and straightforward."—*Weekly Times and Echo.*
" Watches of the highest quality."—*News of the World.*
" Never been surpassed."—*Bournemouth Guardian.*

114

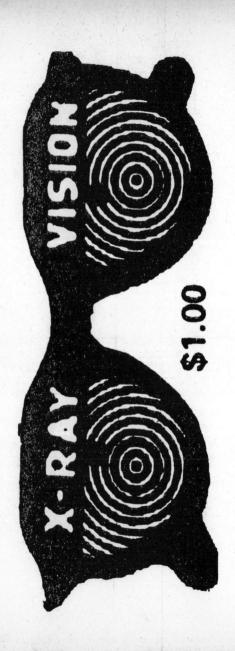

X-RAY VISION

YOU WON'T

BELIEVE YOUR EYES

X-RAY SPECS

An Hilarious Optical Illusion 1^{00}

Scientific optical principle really works. Imagine — you put on the "X-Ray" Specs and hold your hand in front of you. You seem to be able to look right through the flesh and see the bones underneath. Look at your friend. Is that really his body you "see" under his clothes? Loads of laughs and fun at parties. Send only $1 plus 25¢ shipping charges

Money Back Guarantee
HONOR HOUSE PRODUCTS CORP.

Greatest illusion of the century! Apparently see bones thru skin, see thru clothes, etc. Amaze and embarrass everyone! Regular size glasses with built-in optical device.

☐ 3762. XRAY Specs Only .... $1.00 per Pair

Portable X Ray Apparatus

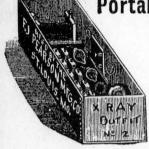

Our No. 2 Outfit for Physicians, Professors, Photographers, and Students. Complete in handsome case, including coil, condenser, 2 sets tubes. battery, etc. Price, $15, net, delivered in U. S. Guaranteed highest class apparatus.

F. J. PEARSON MFG. CO.
Main & Locust Sts.,
St. Louis. Mo.

THE HUMAN HAND WONDER-TUBE

as seen through the

X-Ray effects shown **without Electricity or Crookes Tube.** Rainbow colors at night. No mirrors used. Price of Tube, 10 cts. by mail.

Wonder-Tube Co., 925 F St., Washington, D.C.

Photo View Knife

No. 1701—Art View Knives. Each knife contains picture of dancing girl or bathing beauty which can be seen through miniature magnifying glass contained in one of the ends of each knife, has two blades, brass lined, assorted stag and celluloid colored handles. Length of knife, when closed, 3 in.

Per dozen.................... **$3.75**

ART VIEW RING

$13⁵⁰

Per gross

French Art View Rings

No. 4512—Made of metal, silver finish; set with one white stone brilliant at extreme top. The mounting contains "views" magnified by small powerful lens. Views include bathing girls, actresses, etc. A remarkable selling novelty item.

Per dozen..............$1.25
Per gross............$13.50

SCARF PINS WITH MICROSCOPIC PICTURES

Pretty Views of Actresses, Models, Bathing (?) Girls, etc.

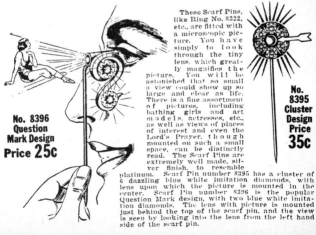

These Scarf Pins, like Ring No. 8322, etc., are fitted with a microscopic picture. You have simply to look through the tiny lens, which greatly magnifies the picture. You will be astonished that so small a view could show up so large and clear as life. There is a fine assortment of pictures, including bathing girls and art models, actresses, etc., as well as views of places of interest and even the Lord's Prayer, though mounted on such a small space, can be distinctly read. The Scarf Pins are extremely well made, silver finish, to resemble platinum. Scarf Pin number 8395 has a cluster of 6 dazzling blue white imitation diamonds, with lens upon which the picture is mounted in the center. Scarf Pin number 8396 is the popular Question Mark design, with two blue white imitation diamonds. The lens with picture is mounted just behind the top of the scarf pin, and the view is seen by looking into the lens from the left hand side of the scarf pin.

No. 8396 Question Mark Design Price 25c

No. 8395 Cluster Design Price 35c

LAUGHING CAMERA. 10c.

The latest invention in Cameras. You look through the lens and your stout friends will look like living skeletons, your thin friends like Dime Museum fat men, horses like giraffes, and, in fact, everything appears as though you were living in another world. Each camera contains two strong lenses in neatly finished leatherette case. The latest mirth-maker on the market: creates bushels of sport.

MY! OH MY!

Catalogue of 1,000 novelties and sample camera 10c., 3 for 25c., 12 for 90c., mailed post-paid. Agents wanted. **Robt. H. Ingersoll & Bro., Dept. No. 85, 65 Cortlandt St., N. Y.**

MAGIC TOY and SUN SPECTACLES.
(Patent Applied For.)

Our attention has been called to this novelty, which is sure to be a popular one. It is brought out by the Hartford Paper Goods Co. of Hartford, Conn., and is both amusing and useful.

As TOY SPECTACLES they provoke "loads of fun." Many laughable changes in expression may be produced by turning the eye-disks to different angles. A small aperture in each disk-centre enables the wearer to see through readily.

As SUN SPECTACLES they are worn reversed, showing only the plain sides of the disks. They thus serve as useful protectors for the eyes against the glare of sun and snow, as the apertures admit only enough light for comfort.

These spectacles retail for **TEN CENTS EACH,** and will be sent postpaid on receipt of price. A liberal discount is offered to the trade.

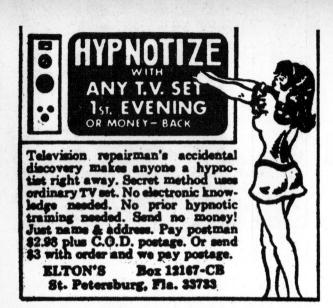
124

AUTOMATIC HYPNOTIZING RECORD

Learn hypnotizing in minutes. Side 1: Self-hypnotism (control bad habits, improve personality, memory, abilities). Side 2: Hypnotizes subject & turns control over to you. Once you hear record, you can hypnotize people without record or any aid except your voice! With book.

☐ 3174. Hypnosis Record $1.95

HYPNOTISM

Would you possess that strange mysterious power which charms and fascinates men and women, influences their thoughts, controls their desires and makes you supreme master of every situation! Life is full of alluring possibilities for those who master the secrets of hypnotic influences; for those who develop their magnetic powers. You can learn at home, cure diseases and bad habits without drugs, win the friendship and love of others, increase your income, gratify your ambitions, drive worry and trouble from your mind, improve your memory, overcome domestic difficulties, give the most thrilling entertainment ever witnessed and develop a wonderfully magnetic will-power that will enable you to overcome all obstacles to your success.

You can hypnotize people instantaneously—quick as a flash—put yourself or anyone else to sleep at any hour of the day or night or banish pain and suffering. Our free book tells you the secrets of this wonderful science. It explains exactly how you can use this power to better your condition in life. It is enthusiastically endorsed by ministers of the gospel, lawyers, doctors, business men, and society women. It benefits everybody. It costs nothing. We give it away to advertise our institution. Write for it today. (Use a letter with a 5-cent stamp.) SAGE INSTITUTE, Dept. 621-B, Rue de l' Isly, 9, Paris VIII, France.

Please mention MAN STORY MAGAZINES when answering advertisements.

KILL THAT CRAVING
STONE DEAD!

DRINK HABIT
CONQUERED

No more misery. Get rid of the drink habit in 3 days.

After being a heavy drinker for years, **I was saved** and providentially came into possession of the true method for overcoming **inebriety**. The drinker who wants to **stop for ever**, getting rid of the awful desire for alcohol, can easily do so, losing no time and enjoying life better than ever before. **Marvellous success.** Safe, reliable, medically endorsed.

Drinkers Secretly Saved.

If a person is addicted so strongly that he has lost desire to be rescued, he can be treated **secretly;** will become disgusted with odour and taste of liquor. Legions of **testimonials** verifying genuineness of my Method. **Joyous news** for drinkers and for **wives, mothers**, &c., contained in my **Book.** Sent, plain wrapper, free. Keep this advt. or pass it on. Address:

EDW. J. WOODS, 10, Norfolk Street (437H), LONDON.

FREE TRIAL
SAVE YOUR FRIEND

Post Free privately.

FROM ITS GRIP.

DRINK·HABIT
SAFELY SECRETLY CURED SURELY

RESCUE YOUR FRIENDS from the drink craving. You can easily do so without their knowledge—secretly, speedily, and harmlessly, with permanent result, at trifling cost. Ample Proofs and **FREE TRIAL** of Fully-guaranteed Treatment sent privately, POST FREE. Correspondence strictly confidential.

THE VENN'S COMPANY,
1, Station Road, Brixton (S. Y.), London

CURE THE DRUNKARD

With or without their knowledge, by a simple and inexpensive Home Method, which can be administered in Tea, Coffee, or Food.

If you have anyone dear to you afflicted by the terrible drink habit, this remarkable drink cure will more than interest you. We will give you positive proof of the wonderful cures effected by this remedy; in fact, we not only tell you, but give an opportunity of testing it free of charge. Even with the trial package we have heard of many who have received benefit. It can be used without fear of detection, and is quite tasteless, and has cured hundreds of cases without the patients' knowledge. A recent testimonial, No. 1353, says:—

"I am happy to be able to tell you now with confidence that a cure has been effected by use of your Antidipso, and the patient is now permanently cured. Since he commenced taking the powders and up to the present time he has had no desire for intoxicants. I am very grateful to you for your help, and will do all I can on your behalf, and will endeavour to get others to try your wonderful and sure remedy." (This testimonial and hundreds of others can be seen at our offices.)

FREE It now rests with you. Write to-day for a free trial, enclosing stamp for postage, and test it for yourself. We will send a free trial, instructions, booklets, and testimonials to all who write to-day. Do it now, to-morrow will bring the remedy. Correspondence strictly confidential.

The WARD CHEMICAL CO., 508, Century House, 205, Regent St., London, W.

128

"I WAS A HUMAN CHIMNEY!"

"TWO years on a lonely gunsite played havoc with my nerves when I was in the A.T.S. To help pass the long hours, I began smoking Soon I was a human chimney. I came back to civvy street a chain smoker, with most of my money going on cigarettes and my eyesight weakened. Now I am told I must either stop smoking or wear spectacles. **But I can't give it up. The craving's too strong. What can I do?**"

Millions would give up cigarettes if they could. Tobacco enslaves both Men and Women. Smoking Ruins your Appearance and Destroys Your Charm. It Literally Burns Money

BANISH THE CRAVING THE EASY WAY
THE "STANDARD" WAY

● Send Stamped, Addressed Envelope, together with 1d. stamp (to cover paper costs in accordance with Government Regulations) for full details of the
STANDARD FOUR DAYS' TREATMENT

THE STANDARD INSTITUTE
(Dept. D.M.) **2, CHURCH STREET, STONE, Staffs.**

133

134

DIG THIS
CRAZY GEAR, MAN!

MAKE THE SCENE WITH THESE FANTASTIC NEW RAVES !

FALSE SIDE PIECES

as seen on T.V

FALSE MOUSTACHE

Send now for these great false sideburns, made in authentic crepe hair. So very realistic, almost undetectable. They attach to the skin and can be used time and time again. Edwardian Style.

Send now for this great false moustache, made in false hair. So very realistic, almost undetectable. Attaches to the skin comfortable to wear, can be used time and time again.

When ordering please send small cutting of your hair for colour matching. Your shade will be matched as near as possible. FIXATIVE FOR THE MOUSTACHE & SIDE PIECES 2/- EXTRA

19/6
SET OF TWO
SEND NOW TO:-

19/6
Post free

PAUL WHITE PRODUCTIONS (Dept.P.S.2),154 Kenyon Lane, Manchester 10

137

Swinging Granny glasses. The latest craze to hit the London scene. Round or oblong, metal framed; tinted sun glasses. **Fab value.**

In crowd Gear. High bulk cotton roll-neck sweaters. Double ribbed neck and cuffs. Black or white. Sizes S, M, L. **Super Value.**

Callers welcome. Send s.a.e. for fabulous FREE fashion catalogue.

CARNABY CAVERN
Dept. (NME), 6 Ganton Street (off Carnaby Street), London, W1

140

141

142

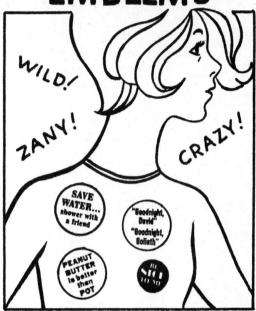
143